Happy 22nd. Anniversary

Ma...

From ...ds

Wendy & Normie

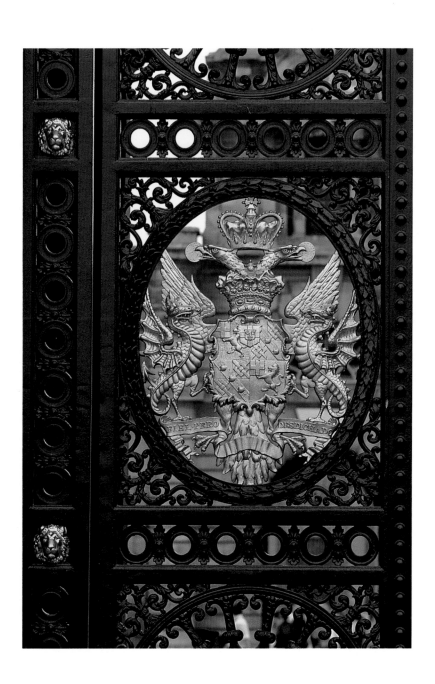

(Page 1) BLENHEIM PALACE, East Gate. The massive entrance gates bearing the Marlborough arms show the pride of a great country house. They also serve a more mundane purpose, hiding the cistern which supplies the kitchen and private apartments. When the Duke is in residence, his flag flies above these gates.

(Pages 2-3) CASTLE HOWARD. When Charles Howard, 3rd Earl of Carlisle, decided to build a house matching his status, he commissioned playwright John Vanbrugh to design it. In his first architectural attempt, aided by Nicholas Hawksmoor, Vanbrugh experimented with a dramatic skyline of domes, cupolas, and lanterns.

(Pages 4-5) CHATSWORTH, Library. The Library of 1830 was once the 1st Duke of Devonshire's Long Gallery. Together with the Ante-Library it contains over 17,000 volumes. An avid book collector, the 6th Duke designed the bookcases.

(Pages 6-7) GILLING CASTLE, Great Chamber. Since 1930, Benedictine monks have run Gilling Castle as the Preparatory School of Ampleforth College. Other country houses have become schools, hotels, and business headquarters. Still more have been demolished; between 1920 and 1955 alone some 400 country houses were destroyed.

(Below) BLENHEIM PALACE. Lead sphinxes on Bleinheim's terraced west front bear the facial features of the 9th Duke of Marlborough's second wife.

Published by Thomasson-Grant, Inc.,
Frank L. Thomasson and John F. Grant, Directors
Designed by Megan R. Youngquist
Edited by Carolyn M. Clark and Elizabeth L.T. Brown
Essays by Timothy O'Sullivan. Edited by Rebecca Beall Barns.
Copyright © 1987 by Thomasson-Grant, Inc. All rights reserved.
Photographs copyright © 1987 by Fred J. Maroon.
Photograph page 137 copyright © 1985 National Geographic Society.
Introduction copyright © 1987 by Mark Girouard.
This book, or any portions thereof, may not be reproduced in any form without
written permission of the publisher, Thomasson-Grant, Inc.
Library of Congress catalog number 86-51535
ISBN 0-934738-25-4
Printed and bound in Japan by Dai Nippon Printing Co., Ltd.
Any inquiries should be directed to the publisher, Thomasson-Grant, Inc.,
505 Faulconer Drive, Suite 1C, Charlottesville, Virginia 22901, telephone (804) 977-1780.

THOMASSON-GRANT

The ENGLISH COUNTRY HOUSE

A Tapestry of Ages

FRED J. MAROON

INTRODUCTION BY MARK GIROUARD

When I went to Chatsworth for Easter, as a six-year-old London child, it never occurred to me that I was staying in a private house. Certainly, when we children walked through the Painted Hall every evening to say good night to my great-aunt, the frescoed ceiling and the balustrade of gilded wrought iron on the gallery along which we walked bore no relationship to any house I had ever visited. I assumed it was some kind of hotel.

But it was not at all frightening or even overpowering. On Easter Sunday, we all went down to the end of the great Canal Pond to look for Easter eggs. These were hard-boiled eggs which had been painted in bright colors and hidden in the long grass on the bank by the ice-house. We scuffled around in the grass hunting for them, while the grown-ups benignly looked on.

Unaccompanied by grown-ups, we ran up and down the long gravel paths lined with statues of Greek and Roman gods and heroes, pointing and giggling at those with exposed private parts. We raced rhododendron leaves against each other in the stream in the Pleasure Grounds. Then back to the temple at the end of the Long Walk. It contained a huge, wire-mesh cage with an arched top like a miniature railway shed, filled with budgerigars. These are associated in my mind with the companionable birds who watched me from my bedroom wallpaper as I went to sleep.

Once our nanny called us over to look out of the window. There, far below and away, along the front of the huge house, was a Rolls Royce. Out of it emerged a bundle of coats and rugs which walked very, very slowly into the house, escorted by a butler and footman. This was all I ever saw of my great-uncle.

The Chatsworth visit was in the late 1930s when English country houses were still largely taken for granted by the families who lived in them. The houses could be very grand, but the life was only occasionally so. At Bowood in Wiltshire, another house where I stayed as a child and boy, I remember best the mixed smell of marble and mackintosh in the Garden Hall. There, what remained of the huge collection of classical statuary assembled by the first Marquess of Lansdowne merged casually with mackintoshes, gumboots, walking sticks, and gardening tools.

Four-poster beds were for use, too. At Hardwick (to which my great-aunt moved when her husband died), the great purple velvet four-poster in the state bedchamber, with its early-17th-century embroidery, was reserved for royal visits. But the others were in frequent use, and very splendid some of them were. I remember saying good morning to my mother, as she ate off her breakfast tray with a frame of 17th-century damask curtains soaring over her to the canopy and ostrich-feather plumes above. It was then that I conceived an ambition to sleep in a four-poster myself. There was a problem, however; one had to be married to qualify, and by the time I was, the beds were no longer available. My great-aunt was dead, Hardwick belonged to the National Trust, the four-posters were roped off and on show to the public.

In between came the 1939-45 war. This was something of a watershed for English country houses. The bigger ones were shut up, or taken over for other purposes. A girls' school was evacuated to Chatsworth; on holidays my sister and I wandered through rows of iron beds in the state rooms, and thumped out "Chopsticks" on school pianos below the frescoed ceilings. Another girls' school moved to Castle Howard; during its tenancy the main block caught fire, and nearly half of it was gutted. When I walked there as a schoolboy from a neighboring school, and toiled along the three-mile avenue, no dome crowned the house as it rose above the lake. Hardwick stood empty all war; the main block of Bowood was occupied till well after the war by the Air Force. This kept it warm in winter, however, probably for the first time in its history. (But it was at Bowood that I had one of the more agreeable experiences of my life, a bath in an old-fashioned, brass-tapped, mahogany-encased bathtub in front of a blazing coal fire.)

After the war, many owners never returned to their country houses, or only returned to a portion of them. In other houses a scaled-down version of the old life, with fewer servants and less elaborate meals, was resumed. When staying with the Duke of Wellington at Stratfield Saye, we still sat in the main dining room, beneath Hoppner's great full-length portrait of the first Duke and his curvetting charger. We ate our soup and meat off his silver plate, and picked at our fruit with gold knives and forks which had belonged to the kings of France. But the food which appeared on the silver plates was not very good. Pike caught by the Duke in the lake was one favorite,

and rook pie another, both handed round the table by a solitary old butler. After dinner, guests were forced to play Scrabble. When there were no guests, the Duke played alone with his librarian — two elderly gentlemen quarrelling over the dictionary in the white-and-gold drawing room, surveyed by the serried ranks of pictures which the first Duke had captured in Spain in the baggage train of Joseph Bonaparte.

It was when staying at Stratfield Saye that I met Rupert Gunnis. At that time, he was working on his great *Dictionary of English Sculptors* and delving into family archives to find who had carved marble chimney-pieces, busts, statues, and church monuments for country-house owners all over the British Isles. He encouraged me to take an active interest in country houses, instead of taking them for granted as places where some of the people I knew lived. It was partly through him that I got a job on the English magazine *Country Life* which in the 1920s had pioneered the serious study of English country houses. I started on a new kind of life, visiting country houses to find who had designed them, made the furniture, carved the stonework, painted the ceilings, and modeled the plasterwork; but also, more and more, to find out how they had been lived in over the centuries.

The keys to all such discoveries were family papers, in accounts, diaries, letters, inventories, household regulations, and so on, from the Middle Ages up till the present day. Some of these had made their way into public collections, but a great deal was still in country houses. If many owners were remarkably casual, and often ignorant, about their possessions, they were even more casual and ignorant about their family papers. Most of them hadn't a clue what they had, and often insisted that they had nothing at all. Looking for papers became an exciting treasure hunt. I had to develop a talent for casually spotting and opening forgotten tin boxes and drawers in dark corners without seeming too inquisitive. It was in this way that I found the complete records of the decoration and furnishing of one great house at the back of a garage, disinterred a selection of medieval deeds wringing wet in an attic above the stables in another, and discovered another lot at the back of a cupboard, mixed up with their owner's hunting boots.

Writing can be hard work, but research is almost pure pleasure, and nowhere more so than in country-house archives. First comes the sense of adventure, when one unties the faded ribbon around a bundle of letters or papers which has not been untied for 100 years or more; then the sense of creation as the facts which the bundles disclose gradu-

Burghley House, Billiard Room, Mr. Simon Leatham and Lady Victoria Leatham.

ally fit together. Bit by bit an outline appears. Then it becomes more than an outline; it becomes the portrait of a house and a family.

I began to appreciate how the relatively informal way in which houses were used in my boyhood was only one chapter in a long story. I learned what an almost unbelievable amount of formality there had been in early country houses: how the chairs where people sat were as carefully tailored to their status as the clothes they wore, and how the business of serving a meal to a great man or getting him up in the morning could be as solemn as a religious ceremony. I learned that beds had not just been places in which to sleep or make love, but formal settings in which to receive important visitors, display mothers and newborn heirs, or lay out corpses on view to mourning tenants and neighbors; and that stairs had not just been means of getting from floor to floor, but pro-  cessional ways up which visiting monarchs in magnificent clothes, or smoking meats on gold or silver plate, were escorted by tribes of servants to the great rooms on the upper floors. I learned about the gradations and rivalries among these servants, and how, whereas in later days the aim was to keep them in the background and create the illusion that everything was done by magic; in earlier days it was to make them as visible as possible, demonstrating the wealth and power of their employers.

I appreciated more and more how country houses were the seats of a ruling class who had to build and foster their image, how carefully devised the training of this ruling class was, and how it changed over the centuries. I read letters describing the Grand Tour, on which young 18th-century aristocrats acquired modern manners and ancient sculpture, with a view to displaying both in their country houses when they returned home. I grew to understand how the magic which still reigns over secret landscapes of houses like Blenheim, Kedleston, and Castle Howard did not come by accident, but was the result of conscious imitation of images and descriptions of Paradise, as it had been envisioned over the centuries.

Of course, I was not alone. Research on every aspect of country houses has been on the increase ever since the war. More and more is

KEDLESTON HALL, Scarsdale family, State Drawing Room.

being discovered all the time about both houses and contents. Discovery is partly fueled by soaring prices. Gone forever are the casual days when sketches by Rubens hung in the gentlemen's lavatory, dogs ate off unrecognized dishes of Ming china, and table tennis was played (as I have played it) in chambers where the ball ricocheted off 18th-century chairs and 17th-century pictures.

Today, when almost all owners only occupy a corner of the bigger houses, it is partly because living in all of them is too expensive, but partly, also, because the contents of the finer rooms have become too valuable to be put to regular use. But in the parts which are lived in, the old combination of style and informality still goes on. In the public rooms, treasures are regularly on show which previously had only been brought out on rare and special occasions. Many country houses are better maintained, better displayed, and better understood than they have been for decades, even if at the cost of a slow but steady sale of their contents, or, more radically, transference from private ownership to the National Trust. The swarms of servants have gone, replaced by live-in couples and relays of "dailies." In their place are the swarms of the public, inside and out, or swarms of children in those considerable numbers of country houses which have become schools. Their days of power are gone for good, but by and large, country houses still play a major role in English life. And they are as beautiful as they have ever been.

All the many aspects of country houses today are brilliantly portrayed by Fred Maroon. He trained as an architect and reacts instinctively to their architectural texture and detail, and above all, to that most vital element of buildings, the quality of light in them. But he is also adept at photographing people, which means not only that he can capture unexpected views of people *in* buildings, but that he can capture the personal quality *of* buildings — the moods of a house, a room, or a garden, which in changing light and weather can be as fleeting as the expressions which cross a human face. Finally, he has never photographed English country houses before. He comes to them like an explorer, and everything is fresh to him. I have been visiting country houses for years, but seeing them again through Fred's eyes I found myself constantly noticing details which I had missed, or being delighted by unexpected angles or perceptive juxtapositions. For those coming to country houses for the first time, I can think of no better or more stimulating visual introduction than his photographs.

MARK GIROUARD

UPPARK, Saloon.

CASTLE HOWARD, Antique Passage.

(Pages 16-17) *HOLKHAM HALL. The 1st Earl of Leicester inherited his fortune at the age of ten. Accompanied by a tutor, he took the Grand Tour of Europe, a customary part of the education of wealthy young men in the 18th century. While traveling, he befriended William Kent and Lord Burlington, also admirers of classical architecture. Together the three designed Leicester's Palladian house, Holkham Hall, atop what was once a treeless slope closely cropped by sheep.*

ICKWORTH. *The 4th Earl of Bristol began building Ickworth in 1795. He intended the Rotunda for living quarters and the two wings for his vast art collection, but the collection was confiscated in Rome during Napoleon's 1798 campaign, and the Earl-Bishop died before Ickworth was completed. When his son finished the house, he reversed the original scheme, using the East Wing as a family residence and the Rotunda for entertaining.*

ASHDOWN HOUSE. Dutch in inspiration, Ashdown looks over the lonely Berkshire downs; tall and narrow, softened by two detached pavilions, it is very unlike other English country houses. The builder, the 1st Earl of Craven, died a bachelor in 1697 at the age of 89. Although they never spoke of love, he spent most of his life in devoted service to Charles I's sister Elizabeth, known as the Winter Queen for the one season she ruled as Queen of Bohemia.

(Above and facing) *MONTACUTE HOUSE. Symmetrical facades, filled with large blocks of windows and a wealth of external details, distinguish the Elizabethan mansion. Montacute, completed in 1601, is considered one of the best-preserved examples. The east front, formerly its main entrance, is the most ornate; carved figures between the top-story windows depict Joshua, David, Judas Maccabaeus, Hector, Alexander, Julius Caesar, Arthur, Charlemagne, and Godfrey of Bouillon.*

(Above and facing) *HOUGHTON HALL, Stone Hall. In 1727, Sir Robert Walpole, first Prime Minister of England, commissioned William Kent to design Houghton's interior as well as the furniture for its state rooms. The Stone Hall is a perfect 40-foot Palladian cube; its pale stone smoothes the transition from exterior to interior. Classical busts of Roman emperors and senators were considered fitting decoration for such a setting. Carvings over the fireplace and doors are by English sculptor John Rysbrack.*

HATFIELD HOUSE, Rainbow Portrait of Queen Elizabeth I *(Courtesy Marquess of Salisbury). In a room just off the Marble Hall hangs this portrait attributed to Isaac Oliver. Eyes and ears cover the Queen's dress, suggesting that through her network of spies she saw and heard everything in the kingdom.*

(Facing) HATFIELD HOUSE, Marble Hall. When Robert Cecil built Hatfield in 1608, his royal ambitions dictated its formal plan. Its two-story Marble Hall connects matching lodgings for the king and queen. The Minstrels' Gallery is crowned by the Cecil crest and family motto Sero Sed Serio, "late but in earnest."

Syon House, Great Hall. Robert Adam, whose neoclassical vision influenced architecture throughout Europe, began remodeling Syon House in 1762. Working within the confines of the old Tudor structure, Adam created a near double cube from the oblong Great Hall by building recesses at each end. He was striving to give the room correct classical proportions; however, the irregularity of these recesses, one semicircular and one rectangular, and the diagonal pattern of ceiling and floor impart a lightness and movement that defied accepted Palladian rules.

SYON HOUSE, *Ante-Room. Adam created a startling contrast between the muted whites of the Great Hall and the vivid colors of the Ante-Room intended as a second hall. Some of the twelve columns topped by solid gilt Ionic capitals and gilded statues were found in the Tiber River. Others are reproductions in scagliola, an imitation marble made of ground gypsum and glue colored with marble dust. The gilded plaster panels of trophies, crafted by Joseph Rose, are decorative descendants of the weapons in medieval halls.*

PENSHURST PLACE, Great Hall. Penshurst vividly evokes the function of the medieval great hall. Here, displaying his generosity and strength, the lord of the house feasted with his household and guests. The lord ate on a dais facing doorways through which servants came bearing the food. Minstrels in the Gallery above accompanied this ceremonial procession with a fanfare. These doorways to the kitchen, buttery, and pantry were later screened to prevent cold air from entering the hall. Among the Great Hall's unusual features are the central hearth, chestnut rather than oak rafters, and the trestle tables, the only surviving examples of their kind.

(Facing) HADDON HALL, Banqueting Hall. From the twelfth century on, owners have enlarged Haddon Hall, adding towers, turrets, and battlements to the once-modest building. The Banqueting Hall, its oldest intact room, was built about 1370. The reconstruction of the roof in 1923-25 required 40 tons of oak timber; a lead box buried in one of the beams preserves details of the restoration for posterity.

(Above and facing) *CASTLE HOWARD, Hall. Rising two stories and topped by a dome, the Hall was designed by Vanbrugh. Italian plasterers introduced rococo elements not popular in England until years later. The paintings are by Venetian artist Pellegrini; unlike the military decorations of medieval halls, many celebrate a musical theme. His dome ceiling painting of Phaethon and the horses of the Sun was destroyed by fire in 1940 and recreated by Canadian artist Scott Medd.*

HOLKHAM HALL, Marble Hall. After the unassuming north front entrance, this magnificent hall, one of the most ornate in England, takes the visitor by surprise. The steps rise from the rustic, the ground floor housing family quarters and service rooms and named for the rusticated stonework on its exterior. William Kent, Lord Burlington, and the Earl of Leicester modeled the Marble Hall after Palladio's design for a Temple of Justice; the fluted columns are copied from the Temple of Fortuna Virilis in Rome, and the vaulted ceiling is after a pattern by Inigo Jones.

(Facing) CHATSWORTH, Painted Hall. Bess of Hardwick and her second husband Sir William Cavendish began building Chatsworth in 1552. Although the floor, stairs, and galleries of the Painted Hall have been altered several times, Louis Laguerre's scenes from the life of Julius Caesar have not been changed since they were painted in 1692-94. Bess' fourth husband was appointed custodian of Mary Queen of Scots and imprisoned her at Chatsworth several times between 1569 and 1584.

CARDIFF CASTLE, *Octagon Staircase. In the peaceful early 15th century, Richard Beauchamp and his wife Isabel moved from the well-fortified Keep into their newly built lodgings. To defend against possible attack, they also erected the Octagon Tower on the Great Hall's northwest corner. Architect William Burges restored the tower in the late 19th century and, by cutting into its thick walls, added the Octagon Staircase. Its bronze and marble newel represents the lion of Scotland.*

ARUNDEL CASTLE, Grand Staircase. Between 1875 and 1900, the 15th Duke of Norfolk renovated the entire castle whose earliest foundations date to the eleventh century. The vaulted stone stairs were among his improvements. On the wall are portraits of the 13th Duke's children.

HAM HOUSE, Great Staircase. The Great Staircase was added between 1637-39. Its balustrade, composed of carved and pierced panels instead of posts, anticipates a style which gained popularity later, after the Restoration. The panels are carved with trophies, ornaments depicting captured weapons. Mathew Goodricke, a decorative artist who worked for the Crown, painted the woodwork to imitate walnut and gilded the carved ornaments.

CRAGSIDE, Staircase. Although the power of the landed upper classes lessened with the rise of the middle class, the new wealthy of the Industrial Revolution strove to imitate them. Sir William Armstrong, inventor and arms dealer, originally built a small weekend retreat of eleven or twelve rooms on a crag above Debdon Burn. Five years later, in 1869, he transformed Cragside into a country mansion run by the world's first domestic hydroelectric power. This staircase was added in 1876; made of oak, its newel posts are fitted with electric lights.

PETWORTH HOUSE, Grand Staircase. Her ambitious grandmother married Elizabeth, heiress to the Percy family's vast estates, to three different men before her 16th birthday. Her third husband, the 6th Duke of Somerset, was known as the "Proud Duke" because of his obsession with his lineage. When Elizabeth came of age in 1688, he began rebuilding Petworth, adding the Grand Staircase painted by Louis Laguerre. On the ceiling is an Assembly of the Gods; on the wall the Duchess rides in a triumphal procession, surrounded by her children and pet spaniel.

(Facing) KNOLE, Great Staircase. Stairs were usually built of stone, turning in broad flights around a square newel until the early 17th century, when improved joinery techniques made open-well wooden staircases popular. Those leading to first-floor rooms of state were splendidly carved and painted. Trompe l'oeil on the walls echo Knole's turned balusters and the leopards holding the Sackville coat of arms. At the foot of the stairs is a statue of Giannetta Baccelli, a celebrated dancer and mistress of the 3rd Duke of Dorset.

GREAT CHAMBERS
AND SALOONS

During the Middle Ages, important houses were built on a rock or a road or a river; in the eleventh century, Windsor Castle became a favorite royal residence because of its commanding position above the Thames and the fact that it was a day's ride from London. Only hunting lodges and later, pleasure houses, belonged in a park. It wasn't until the 1600s that wealthy Englishmen built their houses deep in the country by preference. Eighteenth-century magnates who inherited houses with large settlements at their gates would move the people out of sight, scent, and sound.

Women and royalty have always led the way with improvements in domestic interiors, and the conditions in early dining rooms probably inspired innovation. Eating in a medieval great hall, for example, could not have been very agreeable to the fastidious; noise, smoke from the central hearth, and relentless deterioration of behavior as the evening wore on caused the ladies to retire from the hall earlier and earlier. By the 14th century, the master and his family began to abandon the hall for day-to-day purposes in favor of the great chamber or "chamber with a chimney," a room that was usually on the first floor and approached by a staircase. By the 16th century, families had altogether retreated from the hall to the chamber, where it was possible to be as formal or intimate as circumstances required.

It was not until the 1570s that the Great Chamber was fitted out for Gilling Castle in north Yorkshire. William Fairfax, the new owner, was clearly anxious to impress his neighbors as well as make his family comfortable. The result is the most elaborate of surviving great chambers. The room was wainscoted in nearly 100 detailed panels of English oak. The windows are filled with painted heraldic glass, and a frieze carries over 370 coats of arms and the family trees of the Yorkshire gentry who visited there. In the northeast corner, a painting of six musicians playing their viols and lutes may indicate Sir William's favorite entertainment.

The transformation of Gilling from castle to pleasure house continued in the early 18th century with the addition of two grandiose wings, including a particularly fine Long Gallery. In many comparable houses at about this time the great chamber was demolished or superseded by a saloon, but not at Gilling. In the 1880s, it was sold to a colliery owner and its future as a family house looked secure. But in 1929, Gilling was stripped of some of its fittings and sold to the Benedictine monks of nearby Ampleforth College, who wanted to relocate their preparatory school. The fittings from the Long Gallery eventually went to the Bowes Museum at Barnard Castle in County Durham; William Randolph Hearst bought every moveable feature of the Great Chamber.

"A fine local craftsman, Robert Thompson, repaneled the bare Chamber walls in English oak and carved several mice in the paneling as his trademark," remembers Father Adrian Convery, headmaster at Gilling. "After Hearst died, the original glass, panels, and painted frieze were discovered in unopened crates. Robert Thompson was so excited when he heard that the panels might be coming back to Gilling that he offered money to help pay for the restoration. He asked to be the one to remove his own paneling so that he could restore the originals in the summer of 1952."

Today the Great Chamber has returned somewhat to the use of the hall it was built to replace, serving as the refectory for 100 schoolboys ages eight to thirteen. Father Adrian Convery has known Gilling as boy and monk for nearly 50 years. He believes that small boys placed in surroundings of great beauty will not, on the whole, abuse them. "Gilling has a civilizing influence on the boys," says Father Convery. "All of them know they are in a special place here, but most of them don't really realize until they have left and grown up just how special it is."

(Above and page 46) *GILLING CASTLE, Great Chamber. Great chambers replaced halls as ceremonial rooms of state in the 16th and early 17th centuries. As their importance grew, so did the lavishness of their decoration; Gilling's Elizabethan Great Chamber is ornamented with imagery tracing genealogies and displaying coats of arms. The English oak paneling and painted glass were stripped from the room and sold to William Randolph Hearst in 1929. They remained in their crates for 23 years before they were restored to their former home.*

HADDON HALL, Great Chamber. This medieval house survives virtually unaltered because it was uninhabited during most of the 18th and 19th centuries. In the early 20th century, the 9th Duke of Rutland made its restoration his life's goal. Covered with plaster for years, the Great Chamber's timbering was revealed when the roof was repaired in 1920-22. The 17th-century Flemish tapestries depict woodland scenes. Some 60 others of Haddon's still-large and impressive tapestry collection were destroyed when the stables where they were stored caught fire.

(Above and facing) *UPPARK, Saloon. A brash and impetuous young man, Sir Harry Fetherstonhaugh frequently entertained the Prince Regent at Uppark. Later he withdrew from society, and at age 71, he married Mary Ann Bullock, his head dairy maid, and sent her to be educated in Paris. Their wedding took place in the Saloon. After his death at age 92, Mary Ann and her spinster sister Frances kept the house as it was in Sir Harry's day. Even the gilding and white paint, now darkened to a soft gray because of a high lead content, are original, dating to around 1770.*

(Above and facing) *HOUGHTON HALL, Saloon.* When William Kent designed matching chairs, stools, and settees for this room, unified decorative schemes were new in England. His use of Utrecht velvet for wall-hangings and upholstery was also innovative. Had Houghton's Saloon been used for dining, as were most saloons before formal dining rooms became customary, Kent would not have used velvet; it might retain the smell of food.

(Above and facing) *BLENHEIM PALACE, Saloon, and approach from the south. Murals by Louis Laguerre who was trained at Versailles adorn the walls of Blenheim's Saloon. In formal houses, long axial vistas extended from the saloon, through the state rooms to either side, and often into the surrounding gardens. A visitor could measure his importance by the distance he proceeded down this axis of honor, the rooms farthest from the saloon being most exclusive.*

SYON HOUSE, Dining Room. *Syon's use as a summer villa rather than as a full-blown country house enabled Robert Adam to implement some of his most progressive ideas. The Dining Room, with its French-inspired gold and white decor, comes third in a sequence of five state rooms. Adam ordered the copies of classical statues that fill its niches. Later, sporting paintings were considered appropriate decoration for dining rooms, suggesting the origins of many country houses as hunting lodges and reflecting the interests of the men who habitually lingered there for after-dinner conversation.*

(Facing) CASTLE HOWARD, *Tapestry Room. This room takes its name from the tapestries of the Four Seasons which now hang along the Grand Staircase. Reynold's* The Gentle Savage *depicts Omai, a South Sea Islander, wearing the bark robes of Tahitian nobility. Brought to England in 1774, he was inoculated for smallpox and returned to Tahiti with gifts of muskets and a barrel-organ.*

BROADLANDS, Dining Room. The Dining Room was designed in 1788 by Henry Holland; the mahogany sideboard and pedestals were made especially for the alcove. Four Van Dyck portraits hang in the room. The most famous is a double portrait of the Stuart brothers, young Royalist cavalry officers killed in the Civil War. Two honeymooning royal couples, the Queen and Prince Philip in 1947, and the Prince and Princess of Wales in 1981, have stayed at Broadlands, home of the late Lord Mountbatten.

LONGLEAT HOUSE, State Dining Room. Family portraits hang against walls covered with goat leather tooled in Cordoba around 1620. Depicting the death of Sir Bevill Grenville in the last charge at Lansdown Hill in 1643, the table's silver centerpiece was made by Garrard in 1837 and weighs nearly 63 pounds.

LONG GALLERIES
AND COLLECTIONS

"*E*very lady who has married into my family and come to live in this house has insisted on at least one substantial improvement to it," says Lord De L'Isle of Penshurst Place in Kent. "When a man marries, he must make the place more comfortable. I call this the conjugal theory of domestic architecture. Fortunately, I had two sensible wives, so their suggestions for improvements were always good. It just depended on whether we had the cash."

William Philip Sidney, Lord De L'Isle, succeeded to Penshurst in 1945 on the death of his uncle, the fourth Lord De L'Isle, who was born during the Crimean War and lived to see Penshurst heavily damaged by bombs during World War II. His nephew was awarded the Victoria Cross in 1944, became a member of Parliament, and later served as a minister during Sir Winston Churchill's last term in office. In the early 1960s, he was Governor General of Australia.

One of the most famous members of the family, the soldier-poet Sir Philip Sidney, was described by his contemporary William Camden as "the great hope of mankind" and by Ben Jonson as "the god-like Sidney." He was master of Penshurst for only a few months in 1586 before dying at the age of 32 in the Netherlands from wounds received fighting the Spanish. Sir Philip's younger brother Robert added a number of refinements to Penshurst, including the mark of a settled and civilized 16th-century house, the Long Gallery. He was more than able to afford such luxuries; he inherited fortunes from two uncles, and both of his wives were heiresses.

Originally, a gallery was a protected walkway between two places, serving the same purpose as the cloisters of the monasteries on whose sites so many English country houses were built. In private houses, the galleries, whether adapted or specially built, were places for exercise in bad weather. The Sidneys built the gallery at Penshurst for exercise and pleasure; windows on three sides give excellent first-floor views of the gardens.

Although a gallery's original purpose did not require any particular furnishings, ample wall space and natural light soon led Elizabethans to hang portraits there. Elizabeth I, her peers, courtiers, and followers had a passion for portraits of their contemporaries, and the gallery was a convenient place to display them. On cold and rainy afternoons, such portraits must have made good subjects for conversation and gossip.

Just as people adorn their offices and homes with signed photographs today, the owners of long galleries hung portraits to entertain and pay tribute to friends and patrons. As he strolled through his gallery, an Elizabethan magnate could look upon the faces of his ancestors, living relatives, and friends, the kings and queens of England, and other noted people of his day, contemplating their virtues and achievements. When Robert Sidney built the gallery at Penshurst, portraits of himself and other members of his family were much sought after for the galleries of other houses.

These days, it can be unsettling to walk with the owner of the house through the gallery in the dim light of a winter afternoon; you may suddenly be startled by an ancestor's cool, reptilian gaze. The Sidneys of Penshurst were, as it happens, a comparatively pleasant-looking family, and some of them were admired for their beauty. Dorothy Sidney, Edmund Waller's "Sacharissa," and ancestor of the Spencers and the Churchills, was born at about the time her family's gallery was being fitted with its detailed oak paneling. The present Lord De L'Isle, who prefers to take his walks in the garden, says, "I think my ancestors had the same problems we do. They were always running short of time and money and were generally arguing with their relations."

PENSHURST PLACE, Long Gallery. The poet Sir Philip Sidney was master of Penshurst for only five months before dying of battle wounds in 1586. When his younger brother Robert succeeded to the estate, he added the Long Gallery. Galleries of the day were hung with portraits so that those walking there for exercise could improve themselves spiritually by contemplating the virtues and vices of the people depicted. Beneath the portrait of Queen Elizabeth I is her leaden death mask, thought to be the work of her miniaturist, Nicholas Hilliard.

(Above and facing) *HARDWICK HALL, Long Gallery. Bess of Hardwick, the richest woman in England after Elizabeth I, was married four times; each marriage improved her social and economic status. In 1590, when she was widowed at the age of 70, she began the construction of Hardwick Hall. Hardwick reflects the hierarchical ascendancy typical of Elizabethan architecture, with servants' quarters on the ground floor, family rooms on the first floor, and rooms of state on the second. Here in the second-floor Long Gallery Bess of Hardwick took her exercise. Thirteen tapestries dictated the room's dimensions; in later centuries, the tapestries were covered with portraits including this one of Elizabeth I.*

HAM HOUSE, Long Gallery. Intended for display and exercise, the Long Gallery has no fireplace and little furniture. A portrait of Charles II hangs above the Japanese lacquer cabinet referred to in a 1679 inventory as "One Indian Cabinet with a gilt frame carved." Chinese and Japanese artifacts were often identified as Indian because they were imported by the East India Company.

(Facing) HAREWOOD HOUSE, Gallery. When Edwin Lascelles built Harewood House in 1759, he hired Robert Adam to design its interior. Thomas Chippendale, born a few miles away, made Harewood's furniture; it was the largest commission of his career, and many of his pieces remain in the house. The Gallery, which crowns Adam's work at Harewood, also reveals Chippendale's hand in the wooden curtain swags carved to imitate festoons of heavy taffeta.

(Above and facing) PETWORTH, *North Gallery. The 3rd Lord Egremont added Petworth's North Gallery to house his father's collection of old masters and classical statues, and his own collection of contemporary British art. In 1824, he built the Gallery's North Bay as a setting for Flaxman's last work,* Saint Michael Overcoming Satan. *Artists who wished to sketch or study were welcome to visit the North Gallery which today is one of the few intact galleries formed by a connoisseur of the late Georgian period.*

(Facing) *HAM HOUSE, Round Gallery. The Countess Dysart inherited Ham House from her father. Her first marriage was a failure; before her husband died, the ruthlessly ambitious Countess shunned him for the Earl of Lauderdale. When she and Lauderdale married in 1672, they immediately began enlarging and embellishing Ham House. After his death, she continued alterations, including the conversion of the then-unfashionable Great Dining Room into the Round Gallery. To do this carpenters removed the ceiling of the Great Hall below and added a balustrade.*

POWIS CASTLE, Long Gallery. The oldest surviving part of Powis Castle dates to 1200, but even this stone stronghold may have replaced an earlier wooden structure. By 1300, the castle probably appeared much as it does today. Sir Edward Herbert bought Powis in 1587, and built the Long Gallery six years later. Among the Long Gallery's sculptures are a set of four Dutch marble putti representing the Elements, and another dressed as Minerva.

CHATSWORTH, *Sculpture Gallery.* The 6th Duke of Devonshire, known as the "Bachelor Duke," spent years collecting paintings, sculptures, and books, and adding rooms in which to display these objects and entertain friends. He built the Sculpture Gallery to house what were then modern works. *The Sleeping Endymion with his Dog by Canova was one of the Duke's most treasured pieces.*

WOBURN ABBEY, Temple of the Graces. Empress Josephine commissioned Antonio Canova to carve The Three Graces, *Zeus' lithe and mirthful daughters. After Josephine's death in 1814, the Duke of Bedford saw the unfinished marble in Rome and wished to buy it, but it had been promised to her son. Canova agreed to make another and later visited Woburn to advise the Duke on its placement. To house it a rotunda lit from above was added to the Sculpture Gallery's west end. The Sculpture Gallery has since been dismantled, but* The Three Graces *still occupy their temple.*

WOBURN ABBEY, Long Gallery. Long galleries resemble cloisters where monks walked for exercise in cold or rainy weather, and suggest the ancient abbeys upon which many country houses were built. Woburn's Long Gallery corresponds to the site of Cistercian cloisters. In it hangs George Gower's Armada Portrait of Queen Elizabeth I, *one of the most important historical paintings in England. The Queen is portrayed as Empress with the world in her hand; scenes behind her depict Drake's attack on the Spanish Armada.*

(Facing) BLENHEIM PALACE, Long Library. Vanbrugh built Blenheim from east to west, housing the family in the East Wing while the rest of the building was under construction. This western room, designed by Vanbrugh as a picture gallery, was one of the last to be finished. The 1st Duchess commissioned Rysbrack's statue of Queen Anne; the Long Library preserves her account of her duties as the Queen's Mistress of Robes, as well as Marlborough's military papers and Sir Winston Churchill's notes for his father's biography.

LONGLEAT HOUSE, Library, Lord Christopher Thynne. The present Longleat Collection of some 30,000 volumes was begun by Sir John Thynne, builder of the house. Thynne possessed 85 books, a considerable number in a time when such contemporaries as Bess of Hardwick owned only six, and Sir William Fairfax, builder of Gilling's Great Chamber, owned 39. In the Middle Ages, literacy was rarely among a great lord's skills, and not until the second half of the 17th century were libraries prevalent. Rare books in the Longleat Collection include Henry VIII's Great Bible of 1541 and two original volumes of Chaucer.

(Facing) WOBURN ABBEY, Library. As books and literacy became more common, libraries developed into comfortable sitting rooms favored by family and guests. Woburn's Library, designed by Henry Holland in 1790, is divided into inviting reading spaces by three screens with fluted columns. Many of the volumes concern natural history and the flora and fauna of the Bedford estates. Above the bookcases hangs a collection of portraits, including Rembrandts and Van Dycks.

DRAWING ROOMS

Sir Robert Walpole, England's first prime minister, financed the building of Houghton in the 1720s entirely out of public funds, with little regard for expense. Houghton's magnificence infuriated Walpole's patron, brother-in-law, and neighbor, Marquess Townshend, who left the district whenever Walpole was at home. "Lord Townshend," wrote Lord Hervey, a friend to both men, "looked upon his own seat at Raynham as the metropolis of Norfolk, was proud of the superiority, and considered every stone that augmented Houghton as a diminution of the grandeur of Raynham."

Walpole only spent a month each year at Houghton, where he held "congresses"—parties for the local gentry and his colleagues in the government. Here, Lord Hervey wrote, they lived "up to the chin in beef, venison, geese, turkeys etc. and generally over the chin in claret, strong beer and punch." This was no place for ladies; they were neither expected nor provided for.

The same might be said of the state rooms of many country houses before the 18th century. Although the wealth of heiresses has always been vital to great English houses and the survival of the English nobility, state rooms do not suggest women's role in the partnership of power.

The drawing room began as a woman's retreat from public pressures. "In earlier days, people lived in a hall, hugger-mugger," says Lord De L'Isle of Penshurst Place. "Later, ladies needed a place they could go to get away from it all, a withdrawing room." Gradually, as formal manners declined in the late 18th century, the appeal of the drawing rooms grew; they came to surpass masculine great chambers and saloons in importance.

Houghton's later history reflects the ways in which women have contributed to the survival of great houses. When Walpole's eccentric grandson inherited Houghton, he ran into debt, sold some of the most important paintings to Catherine the Great of Russia, and allowed the house to fall into disrepair. The house eventually passed to the Cholmondeleys, the family into which Walpole had married his daughter. This ancient English family derives its name from their home in Cheshire. The name, pronounced "Chumley," is a notorious stumbling block, especially for foreigners. The only other name to compare is that of Marjoribanks, pronounced "Marchbanks." Describing the difficulty of pronouncing English names, an American once told his friends that he had met someone who spelled his name C-H-O-L-M-O-N-D-E-L-E-Y and pronounced it "Marchbanks."

During the agricultural depression of the 1880s, Houghton was put on the market, but no one bought it. As often happens, new blood revived the fortunes of the house. In 1913, the heir to the fourth Marquess of Cholmondeley married Sybil Sassoon, the daughter of a merchant family that was well known in European society.

With her husband, Sybil restored the house to its present condition; most of the original furnishings, dating from the time of the first prime minister, are still in place and in good repair. They brought in paintings from the Cholmondeley and Sassoon family collections to replace some that had been sold in haste by Walpole's grandson.

In 1973, Lady Cholmondeley restored Houghton's west front steps as a tribute to her husband. (The steps had been demolished by Walpole's grandson because he couldn't afford to repair them.) "Of course my husband and I had both of us been very keen to do it the whole of our time at Houghton," says Lady Cholmondeley. "But it was rather expensive, and then later on the Government wouldn't give us planning permission, which was rather strange. So after my husband died, I decided to do it as a memorial to him."

HOUGHTON HALL, Common Parlour. John Singer Sargent came out of retirement in 1913 to paint this portrait of the Countess of Rocksavage, now the Dowager Marchioness of Cholmondeley, for her wedding present. When Lady Cholmondeley was a child, Sargent, a close friend of her mother, often played piano duets with her and took her for drives.

HOUGHTON HALL, White Drawing Room. Most of Robert Walpole's extraordinary paintings, including several which hung in this room, were sold to Catherine the Great by his grandson, an eccentric who in fits of insanity allowed the house to fall into disrepair. The works now form the core collection of Leningrad's Hermitage Museum. A study in white, the White Duck *is considered French painter J.B. Oudry's masterpiece, and is one of the many paintings at Houghton which belong to Lady Cholmondeley's family.*

BURGHLEY HOUSE, Brown Drawing Room. Drawing rooms began as "withdraughtes" or "draughtes,"small rooms attached to chambers and used as private eating, sitting, and reception areas. Until the end of the 16th century, servants often slept in them, close to their masters' chambers. The Chippendale mirror reflects a bed used by Queen Victoria as a child when she visited Burghley with her mother.

(Facing) BLENHEIM PALACE, *Red Drawing Room. As country house owners began to spend less time in their own state apartments, smaller and more numerous common rooms, especially drawing rooms, grew popular. Because women customarily withdrew to drawing rooms while men remained in the dining room to talk, smoke, and drink, they were decorated in what was considered a feminine style. Commissioned to hang in the Red Drawing Room opposite a group portrait by Reynolds, Sargent's* Marlborough Family *depicts the 9th Duke, his wife, and children.*

BLENHEIM PALACE, *First State Room. Three apartments known as the First, Second, and Third State Rooms connect Blenheim's Saloon and Long Library; all contain tapestries depicting Marlborough's military campaigns. Over the mantel hangs Carolus Duran's portrait of the 9th Duchess of Marlborough, Consuelo Vanderbilt, at age 17. An American heiress, she rocked her son the 10th Duke in the Italian cradle given to her by her mother.*

ICKWORTH, Drawing Room. The four rooms in Ickworth's Rotunda, the Hall, Drawing Room, Library, and Dining Room, were used for entertaining and for housing the 1st Marquess of Bristol's collections. Many Hervey family portraits hang in the Drawing Room completed in the 1820s. The pier glass and table are 18th-century Portuguese; the glass wall sconces were added to the room in 1910 by the 4th Marquess.

KEDLESTON HALL, State Drawing Room. Third in a succession of architects hired by Sir Nathaniel Curzon to build Kedleston in the 1750s, Robert Adam hardly altered his predecessor's plan for the Drawing Room. Adam's original chaste design for the room's four monumental sofas was more freely interpreted. Greatly enlarging the pieces, cabinetmaker John Linnell substituted Adam's draped caryatids with merman and mermaid supports. The matching upholstery and wall-hangings are copies of the original.

(Above and facing) CRAGSIDE, Drawing Room. Since Cragside's Southeast Wing is dominated by a massive central heating system, its only large room is the Drawing Room begun in 1883. Its placement far from the bedchambers or dining room marks a complete metamorphosis from the drawing room's original function. During the 1st Lord Armstrong's time, only turf was burned within the ten-ton, two-story chimneypiece.

(Pages 88-89) *BURGHLEY HOUSE, Heaven Room. This is considered Verrio's masterpiece, the only room he ever painted from ceiling to floor. Completed in 1694, it depicts scenes from classical mythology. Verrio painted himself on the east wall as Dante at Vulcan's forge. As part of a five-room suite prepared for a proposed visit from George IV when he was Prince of Wales, the Heaven Room is sometimes called the Fifth George Room. During her stay here, Queen Victoria used it as a breakfast room.*

OMNIA VINCIT AMOR ET NOS CEDAMVS AMORI

(Above and facing) *CARDIFF CASTLE, Winter Smoking Room. Roman legions built a fort on Cardiff Castle's strategic site near the Bristol Channel as early as 54-68 A.D. Beginning in 1865, the 3rd Marquess of Bute transformed the existing castle into what is essentially a Victorian fantasy of medieval splendor. Architect William Burges added the Clock Tower on the site of a Roman bastion. Its suite of bachelor apartments includes the Winter Smoking Room where, following Victorian custom, men donned elaborate smoking jackets to enjoy cigars, liquor, and conversation.*

BURGHLEY HOUSE, *Black and Yellow Bedchamber. The term "bedchamber" was not used until the mid-16th century; prior to this time chambers also served a variety of less private functions including eating, entertaining, and doing business. As bedchambers gained in prominence, the bed became a symbol of wealth, rank, and power. This room takes its name from the richly embroidered black satin hangings lined with yellow that grace the windows and the Queen Anne state bed.*

(Facing) HAM HOUSE, *Queen's Closet. The Queen's Closet, prepared for Charles II's wife in the 1670s, is the last and most private in a series of state rooms; only intimates of the Queen or the Lauderdales were received here. From the ceiling painting attributed to Verrio to the marquetry floor inlaid with the Lauderdales' initials, this small room is astonishingly rich in detail. The fireplace surround and windowsill are of scagliola, an imitation marble whose use in England was extremely rare at the time. The sleeping chair reclines; its original silk covering matches the wall-hangings.*

(Facing) POWIS CASTLE, State Bedroom. Around 1661, Charles II's practice of admitting people to his withdrawing room and even to his bedchamber set a new style. Although English bedchambers never became as public as French ones, their sumptuous decor reflects their importance as reception rooms. The placement of the 18th-century mahogany bed behind a railed recess in Powis' State Bedroom is the only surviving English example of a typically French arrangement. The bed and Queen Anne chairs of silvered gesso are covered in Spitalfields velvet.

KNOLE, King's Room. Among the rarities in the King's Room are the state bed covered with gold and silver brocade and the set of silver furniture. In baroque bedrooms, a matching table, looking glass, and candlesticks usually stood against the pier, or wall between windows. As ladies and gentlemen began to perform their toilettes in dressing rooms or closets, these furnishings became less functional and more elaborate. Since 1701, the looking glass has hung against a 17th-century tapestry depicting the story of Nebuchadnezzar.

(Facing) *WOBURN ABBEY, Queen Victoria's Bedroom. Intended for visiting royalty, Woburn's state apartments were seldom occupied. When not in use, they were shuttered and the furniture was covered. This practice accounts for the good condition of the bedroom completely redesigned during the 4th Duke's renovations of 1747. Queen Victoria and Prince Albert stayed here in 1841.*

WOBURN ABBEY, Queen Victoria's Dressing Room. Often as large as bedchambers, dressing rooms sometimes served as private sitting rooms. Before Queen Victoria's visit, this room was used as a drawing room. In it hangs a collection of 17th-century Dutch and Flemish paintings, including Aelbert Cuyp's Nijmegen on the Vaal *over the rolltop desk made in 1774.*

CHATSWORTH, State Bedroom. The 1st Duke of Devonshire's love of building brought many alterations to Chatsworth in the late 17th century. One of his undertakings was to build state rooms in what was once the Elizabethan Long Gallery. Although it was not until Queen Victoria's reign that a monarch ever visited, these splendid rooms were designed for the reception of royalty. Stamped and gilded leather covers the walls; the allegorical ceiling painting by Laguerre shows Dawn banishing Night. The state bed belonged to George II and was given to the 4th Duke upon the King's death.

SERVICE ROOMS

When the fifteenth Earl of Derby died in 1893, 727 servants and retainers were remembered in his will. A great medieval nobleman would have been proud of so large an establishment. However, since the two World Wars, the size of households has withered. Still, even today, with the help of every modern appliance, the largest houses need about 40 full-time staff.

When newcomers join the staff, they usually leave within 24 hours or stay forever; most houses have one or two employees whose families have worked there for over a century. At Burghley House in Lincolnshire, the retired chauffeur Walter Barnes recalls that the fifth Marquess of Exeter made the same speech every year at the Christmas party, saying, "We are one big, happy family." In a way, they still are.

Jim Curtis, who worked at Burghley for 50 years, was born two miles away in the village of Barnack where stone was quarried for the house during the 16th and 17th centuries. His father had been a watchman at Burghley, but it was an uncle, the butcher there, who brought Jim to the staff in 1934 as temporary Steward's Room boy at the Exeters' London house during the "Season." His first duties were "learning how to clean shoes, how to valet, how to wait at table." As he says, "My heart was in it. I wanted to be in service, and I took to it." Before Jim returned from London, the butler reported to his counterpart at Burghley, "He's getting on so well he'll soon be ready to go in the dining room." This signaled that Jim might make a footman and wear the Burghley livery with its ranks of silver buttons around the edges of the tail coats.

Back at Burghley, Jim joined a live-in indoor staff of 20, in a rigid hierarchy with the butler at the top and Jim at the bottom. At meals men sat down one side of the table and women down the other, with the butler, cook, lady's maid, sewing maid, and head housemaid retiring to a separate room for dessert. The food was always excellent: "If there was pheasant in the Dining Room, there was pheasant in the Servants' Hall too," Jim recalls, and all the fresh fruit and vegetables were grown in Burghley's hothouses and walled kitchen garden. Discipline as well as service was expected in return. The fifth Marquess of Exeter presided at prayers in the Chapel every morning at 9:15; no excuses for absence were accepted. The junior staff needed a pass from the butler to stay out after nine in the evening, and were required to tell him where they were going, who they were going to see, and to sign in when they returned. This rule did not stop Jim from courting and marrying a girl on the staff who later became lady's maid.

Jim Curtis looks back with special pride on the 25 years he was butler to the sixth Marquess of Exeter, who won an Olympic gold medal for hurdling in 1928 and later served as Governor of Bermuda. The Marquess brought to Burghley a range of guests whose variety had not been known there since William Cecil started building the house in the 16th century. It was Jim's duty to make sure that the guests, usually limited to parties of about 20 by the size of the dining room table, enjoyed the full comforts of the house. An individual's particular requirements were announced in advance; rubber magnate Harvey Firestone needed to be supplied almost continuously with cups of tea, while John Paul Getty insisted upon food prepared without salt.

Today Jim Curtis lives in a cottage in Burghley's Courtyard. Although retired, he often goes over to the house on weekends and special occasions to help his successor whom he trained for twelve years. Standing in the Great Hall, beside what is reputedly the largest silver wine cistern in existence, which takes four men to move and used to take Jim and a colleague three hours to clean, he reflects, "This was a very happy house, very happy. My wife and I could not have had a more lovely lord and lady than the late marquess and his wife. We've had a wonderful time here."

(Above and pages 104-105) *BURGHLEY HOUSE, Old Kitchen. The Kitchen is one of Burghley's earliest rooms. Its high, vaulted ceiling was typical of architectural attempts to reduce the heat, smell, smoke, and dirt of cooking on an open fireplace. A painting of an ox carcass, attributed to Rubens, hangs on the west wall; over 260 copper utensils are displayed throughout the kitchen.*

UPPARK, Dairy. Until the 17th century, country houses were usually built in valleys to assure that they were readily accessible by road in winter and easily supplied with water throughout the year. Sir Edward Ford, whose house at Uppark sat upon an imposing hill, invented the first effective water pump in 1650, ending the drudgery of drawing water by hand from deep wells. At the end of a private terrace is the elegant tiled dairy where Mary Ann Bullock worked before she married Sir Harry Fetherstonhaugh in 1825.

(Facing) UPPARK, Butler's Pantry. Medieval noblemen served as administrators, secretaries, bodyguards, and servants in country houses, but when the size of households decreased, so did the status of household service. As women assumed many jobs formerly performed by men, the butler's supervisory role over the remaining male servants increased in importance. The Butler's Pantry at Uppark illustrates his various duties, among them washing glass, serving wine, and caring for the gentleman's hunting habit.

ERDDIG, *Dry Laundry. The owners' wives and daughters, their companions and nurses, and an occasional laundress were the only women in medieval households. As the status of servants declined, women were hired to cook and clean. At Erddig, the laundry yard constructed in the early 1770s was the preserve of the female staff. With the turn of a handle, the original box mangle in the Dry Laundry trundles a box of stones over wooden rollers, pressing the clothes laid beneath them.*

ERDDIG, Servants' Hall. Beginning in the late 18th century, Erddig's owners commissioned portraits of their staff. The resulting collection provides an unprecedented record of the complex social history of this country house. Ten of these portraits hang in the Servants' Hall, whose ceiling is decorated with radiating swords, trophies of the Denbighshire Militia. Servants' halls came into use in the second half of the 17th century after household staff stopped taking their meals in the great hall.

CHAPELS

After knowing Chatsworth for nearly 50 years, the Duchess of Devonshire still finds quicker routes between rooms on different floors. This is hardly surprising; Chatsworth has 175 rooms, 3,426 feet of passages, 17 staircases, and 359 doors.

The Duchess never expected to live in such a house, nor indeed to be a duchess. Born Deborah Mitford, she is the youngest of the second Lord Redesdale's celebrated daughters; her sisters are Nancy, Jessica, Diana, Pamela, and Unity. In 1941, she married Andrew Lord Cavendish, the younger son of the tenth Duke of Devonshire. Her husband became heir to the dukedom when his childless brother was killed in action in World War II. The sudden death of the tenth Duke in 1950 left Andrew and his young wife to take over at a bleak time in the history of English country houses. Four-fifths of their inheritance went for death duties.

The Devonshires were comfortable in a relatively modest 18th-century house nearby at Edensor when the Chatsworth agent, Hugo Read, inspired them to move. "There's that house. You have got to look after it whatever happens. Somebody has got to see that the windows are opened and so on. Why don't you go and live in it?" The Duchess was drawn to the house: "It seemed so sad to have this marvelous place and just visit it."

Chatsworth, little altered or improved since before World War I, had been described as exuding "a feeling of extreme melancholy for things vanished and remote." The Chapel, painted by Verrio and carved by a student of Grinling Gibbons, was one of the first formal rooms to be finished and has hardly been altered since. The presence of a chapel in so many great houses recalls the ecclesiastical origins of a large portion of their owners' fortunes: the acquisition of land from monasteries dissolved in the 16th century, and rewards bestowed by William of Orange for help in displacing the Roman Catholic James II from the throne in 1688.

For generations, many noblemen kept their own chaplain who doubled as tutor to the sons of the house. More recently, the chapels have been served by a priest from a nearby parish. Sometimes worship in country house chapels carries a hint of the bizarre. At Blenheim, where Rysbrack's tomb for the first Duke of Marlborough fills most of one side of the chapel, it has always seemed that one might be worshipping the Duke rather than God. At another house, an owner habitually answered the parson's exhortation "Let us pray" with "By all means." In recent years, when it has been difficult to find rites conducted according to the *Book of Common Prayer*, the control of a chapel has been a comfort to those who prefer a more traditional service. "Fortunately," one owner has remarked, "I have a private chapel, so there is no dispute over what form of service is used."

Until 1914, most country house chapels had daily prayers as well as Sunday rites. Until 1939, it was commonplace for the whole household to attend at least one weekly service. The seating arrangement of the congregation was divided: men from women, masters from servants, upper servants from lower servants. At Chatsworth, the youngest children sat in the gallery with their nannies, recalls the Duchess of Devonshire, and a child sometimes managed "to push a prayer book over the ledge to crash on the floor below and make a welcome diversion."

With a few exceptions, such as Hatfield where services are arranged whenever the family is at home, country house chapels today are used mainly for christenings or weddings, and for Easter or Christmas. For the last, most chapels are now far too small. The Christmas carol service at Burghley is always booked by September, and at Chatsworth it has become so popular that it will have to be moved from the Chapel to the Painted Hall.

CHATSWORTH, Chapel. Painted with scenes from the life of Christ, the Chapel has not been altered since its completion in 1693. Verrio's Doubting Thomas surmounts the altar-piece carved of local alabaster. The fragrance of the cedar wainscot pervades the room.

HATFIELD HOUSE, Chapel. In 1835, a fire broke out in Hatfield's West Wing. Although fire engines from London arrived late, luckily huge leaden cisterns on the roof melted, water doused the exterior, the wind changed, snow began to fall, and the Chapel was saved. Its ground floor was remodeled between 1869 and 1880; the Flemish stained-glass windows are from the original building of 1608.

(Facing) HADDON HALL, Chapel. The Chapel contains features dating from almost every period in Haddon's building history. In recent years, medieval wall paintings faded to soft grays were discovered under a coat of whitewash. Some of the paintings imitate contemporary tapestries; others depict events from the lives of Saint Christopher and Saint Nicholas. The white marble effigy was modeled by the 8th Duchess of Rutland as a memorial to her son Lord Haddon who died at the age of nine.

CASTLE HOWARD, Mausoleum. Nicholas Hawksmoor's modesty throughout his collaboration with Vanbrugh on Castle Howard and Blenheim makes pinpointing his specific contributions difficult. Hawksmoor's design for the Mausoleum, conceived primarily as a visual component of the landscape, is entirely his own. Confined in London by crippling gout during its construction, he did not live to see the Mausoleum finished.

THE GROUNDS

*B*efore the triumph of the landscape movement in 18th-century England, landowners who created gardens could expect to see them mature within their lifetimes. Seventeenth-century diarist John Evelyn noted that Penshurst Place in Kent was already famous for its gardens and fruit. Over the next two centuries, the gardens must have gone to seed, because they had to be completely replanted. In the early 1800s, they were recreated in the formal style of the 17th century, with terraces, *allees*, and a boxwood parterre trimmed into precise blocks. Bombs severely damaged the gardens during World War II, but the present Lord De L'Isle restored them again after the war.

As styles changed, fashion-conscious landowners often completely uprooted and replanted gardens that were just starting to mature. Sometimes neglect has been the secret of a garden's survival. In the early 17th century, the first Earl of Salisbury planted a garden at Cranborne Manor in Dorset. As he prospered, he became involved in developing a garden on his other estate, the more palatial Hatfield House, which was to be the Salisbury family's main residence for more than 200 years. The second Marquess of Salisbury rediscovered the delightful gardens at Cranborne in the 1860s and restored them. The formal framework and subdivision of the garden into "rooms," a style used with legendary effect at Sissinghurst in Kent, had been preserved remarkably well for two centuries.

In the 18th century, the pursuit of pleasure ruled garden design. Some gardens were laid out in circuits, with exotic buildings — pagodas, rotundas, temples, Chinese dairies — at suitable intervals. Visitors could enjoy diversions ranging from fishing to cold baths to simple relaxation. By 1760, the circuit at Stowe in Buckinghamshire had more than 30 different buildings along it.

It was at Castle Howard that the 18th-century English landscape movement really hit its stride. The third Earl of Carlisle directed George London and Henry Wise to design formal gardens around the new house, while Lord Carlisle set about creating an idyllic scene to the southeast that could be translated, without embellishment, to a canvas of Claude. The lakes, woods, and serpentine river form a landscape that is heightened by Vanbrugh's Temple of the Four Winds, a Grand Bridge, and finally the Mausoleum designed by the English baroque architect Nicholas Hawksmoor. Horace Walpole once said that the Mausoleum would "tempt one to be buried alive."

There was, perhaps, a golden age earlier in the 20th century when the great manmade landscapes were in their prime, an Arcadian world superbly evoked in Evelyn Waugh's novel *Brideshead Revisited*. The use of Castle Howard as Brideshead in the television version of the novel made such a powerful impression that tourists quite often ask when the Howards bought the house from the Marchmains. "The program showed the opulence of England in the 1920s and '30s, so it didn't really give an idea of what life is like today in an English country house," explains Simon Howard, who became the custodian when his father died in 1984.

"We continue to plant the gardens at Castle Howard with a vision of Paradise in mind," adds Simon Howard, who rode his bicycle through the gardens as a boy and now walks through them for exercise and contemplation. The gardens also supply the house with food and flowers; Mrs. Howard does all the floral arrangements. The young custodian is not a gardener himself. "I am not a green-fingered man," he explains. "I seem to touch things, and they fall over."

"There is immense theater in the design of the house and its landscape. When I was a boy, the Mausoleum was awe inspiring. It exuded something different, and I felt fear. The building is a great testament to death." Lord Carlisle and some of his descendants are buried there; Simon Howard hopes to be buried there, too.

HATFIELD HOUSE. When Henry VIII dispossessed the Catholic Church, he took over the Old Palace, now Hatfield, as a residence for his children. Queen Elizabeth I spent her childhood here, sharing the education of her younger brother Edward. At the age of 25, while reading under an oak tree in the park, she first received word of her accession to the throne. Her successor, James I, did not like the Old Palace and traded it for Theobalds, residence of his Chief Minister, Robert Cecil, who built Hatfield on this site in 1608.

(Above and facing) *CHATSWORTH. The 6th Duke of Devonshire replaced damaged Cibber marble statues with copies, and his gardener Joseph Paxton transformed the neglected gardens, giving them their present form. Twenty-three-year-old Paxton first arrived at Chatsworth on May 9, 1826, at 4:30 a.m. After climbing the wall to look at the garden, he put the men to work, went in to breakfast with the housekeeper, and immediately fell in love with her niece whom he married the following year.*

PENSHURST PLACE, Lord De L'Isle and the head gardener. The south front of the house looks as it did in 1346 when Sir John de Pulteney, a wool merchant and four-time mayor of London, lived here. Before Penshurst was completed, Sir John's steward reported that fruit and vegetables were already planted in the garden, today enclosed by yew-hedged walks.

POWIS CASTLE. *Designed in the late 17th century, Powis' terraced formal gardens are attributed to William Winde. His design, based on that of 16th-century Italian palace gardens, reflects the owner's rank and power. Powis' is one of the few formal gardens to have escaped alterations by "Capability" Brown and his followers, who in the late 18th century revolutionized English garden design with their naturalized landscapes. Four lead pastoral figures and two urns punctuate the balustrade in front of the Orangery's 18th-century sash windows.*

BLEINHEIM PALACE, Italian Garden. For the 1st Duke of Marlborough, gardener Henry Wise planted a formal "military" garden, and for the Duchess, he planted a flower garden visible from her bow window. On the site of her garden, the 9th Duke created the Italian Garden. Its centerpiece, the Mermaid Fountain, was carved by expatriate American artist Waldo Story, who also modeled busts of the 9th Duke and Duchess.

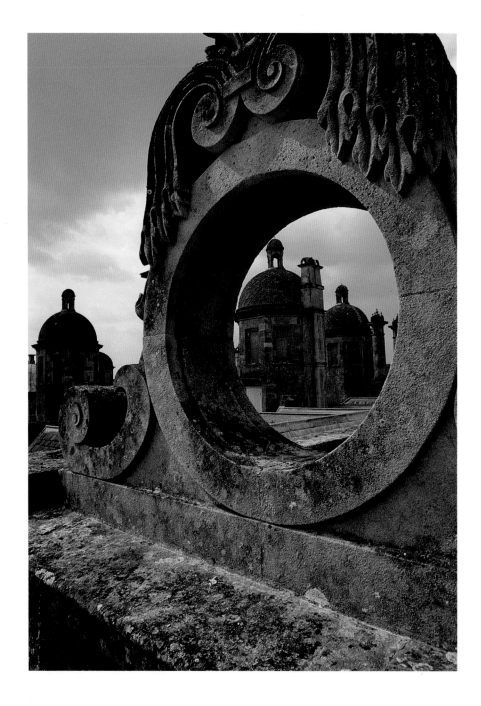

LONGLEAT HOUSE. *Wine, fruit, and spiced sweets offered while dinner dishes were removed before the evening's entertainment came to be known as "dessert" after the French verb meaning "to clear the table." When served in a special tower on the roof or in the garden, these intimate, after-dinner repasts were called "banquets." Sir John Thynne so enjoyed the climb and view a banquet on a friend's roof afforded that he scattered Longleat's roof with square and octagonal banqueting turrets.*

BURGHLEY HOUSE. *Elizabethans delighted in witty, unusual, and elaborate analogies and in physical expressions of the mind's ingenuity. Burghley's ornate roof with its domed turrets topped with gilt weather vanes, chimneys surrounded by lofty Doric columns and cornices, and balustrade adorned with the Cecil crest, is an architectural expression of the 16th-century passion for visual metaphors.*

SEZINCOTE, Susanna and David Peake and their daughter Katharine. Hired by his brother Charles, Samuel Cockerell, Surveyor to the East India Company, built Sezincote with the aid of Thomas Daniell, an artist who had recently spent ten years in India. Their design for the house was inspired by the Mogul ruler Akbar who, in one of his attempts to integrate his diverse country, combined Hindu and Islamic architectural elements. Sir Charles Cockerell slept in the Octagonal Room decorated to resemble a tent with wooden spears supporting a canopy.

FLINTHAM HALL, Squire Myles Hildyard. Thomas Blackborne Thoroton inherited Flintham and little else. Although his father's land purchases left the family deeply in debt, Thoroton lived like a wealthy man. In 1853-57, he had his grandfather's original stucco house of 1798 totally encased in stone. (Page 130) Flintham's two-story conservatory, notable among his embellishments, exemplifies the mid-Victorian taste for ornate, glass-enclosed additions.

(Above and page 132) *HOLKHAM HALL. Holkham's builder, Thomas Coke, admired and collected classical art, but unlike most powerful landlords who left agricultural pursuits to their tenants, he also farmed part of his own estates. At his annual sheep shearings, local farmers learned new techniques. Today's country fairs at Holkham benefit several charities. Among the participants is the first regiment of* Grenadiers à Pied de la Garde Imperiale, *formed to rekindle interest in the military history of the Napoleonic era.*

CHATSWORTH, *Country Fair.* Ever since it was built, Chatsworth has been open to the public. In 1844, the 6th Duke of Devonshire ordered that anyone who asked be given a complete tour of the house and a full demonstration of the waterworks. When the Midland Railway made Chatsworth easily accessible for the first time in 1849, 80,000 people came to see the house that summer.

LONGLEAT HOUSE. Excluding family, medieval households often numbered well over 100 people, but as the Tudor monarchs replaced rule of force with rule of law, such numerous retainers became an expensive anachronism. Remnants of the old system in which household service was a route to fortune lingered until the early 17th century. Profits earned as steward to the Duke of Somerset enabled Sir John Thynne to build the great Renaissance house Longleat, beginning in 1568.

Burghley House, Horse Trials. Known as "Lord Burghley the Olympic Hurdler" for his 1928 Olympic Gold Medal in the 400-yard hurdles, the late Marquess of Exeter initiated the Burghley Horse Trials. The Three Day Event subjects horses and riders to various tests of their skill and stamina: dressage, cross-country jumping, and stadium jumping.

PENSHURST PLACE. As the Victorian dinner hour grew later, ladies surreptitiously made a meal of afternoon tea and cakes served in their bedrooms. The practice gradually became more popular and moved to the drawing room. By the end of the century, both sexes enjoyed an elaborate five o'clock tea in the drawing room or on the lawn when weather permitted.

(Pages 138-139) ARUNDEL CASTLE. The 1st Earl of Arundel received his title on Christmas of 1067, and it was he who first built on Arundel's site overlooking the Sussex coast. Dominating the surrounding town, the house was reconstructed and restored by the 15th Duke of Norfolk; all that remains of the 1st Earl's structure is the stone Keep. Nearby Arundel Cathedral enshrines the remains of Saint Philip Howard, 13th Earl of Arundel, who was canonized in 1970. He died while imprisoned in the Tower of London, accused of having a Mass said for the success of the Spanish Armada.

HOUGHTON HALL. A man's ambitions could be judged by the type of country house he built. When Robert Walpole rose from a family of minor gentry to a position of prominence, he bought land, engaged the best architects and craftsmen to begin building Houghton in 1721, and filled the house with a fine art collection. His brother-in-law and neighbor Lord Townshend, who had launched Walpole's success, was exceedingly bitter. He viewed Houghton as a diminution of his own estate, and left the neighborhood whenever Walpole entertained there.

(Pages 142-143) *KEDLESTON HALL. When Sir Nathaniel Curzon inherited Kedleston, he found it inadequate to house his collection of paintings and had it torn down. To clear the site for a new house and landscape the park, he followed 18th-century custom and moved the village of Kedleston over half a mile from its original location. Only the church stands where it did before Curzon began building in 1759.*

CHATSWORTH. *The 1st Duke of Devonshire remodeled the house built by his ancestor Bess of Hardwick, adding state rooms and, as was common in baroque houses, different facades for each elevation. The 4th Duke's decision that the house be approached from the west required moving the stables and offices, razing the cottages of Edensor village, altering the course of the River Derwent, and building a new bridge.*

144